WATER FOR GOD'S
SONS
AND
DAUGHTERS

CORBETT GOURIE

WestBow Press books may be ordered through booksellers or by contacting:

WestBow Press
A Division of Thomas Nelson & Zondervan
1663 Liberty Drive
Bloomington, IN 47403
www.westbowpress.com
1 (866) 928-1240

ISBN: 978-1-5127-7714-7 (sc)
ISBN: 978-1-5127-7715-4 (e)

Library of Congress Control Number: 2017903260

Print information available on the last page.

WestBow Press rev. date: 03/06/2017

WESTBOW
PRESS®
A DIVISION OF THOMAS NELSON
& ZONDERVAN

Acknowledgments

I would like to thank my Lord, Jesus Christ, for giving me the ability to write this book and for casting away all my fears and doubts.

I want to thank my wife for supporting me through every step. My mom who through all my life has been an example of unwavering faith and persistence and to my pastor Joaquin Garcia for always being there for me.

Also to all the people who have been in my life and in some way have shaped me into the man I am today.

My deep gratitude to the many people who saw me through this book; to all those who provided support, offered comments and assisted in editing, proofreading and design.

I thank you with all my heart.

God bless you!

Contents

Truth

The Lord created heaven and the earth

then He made Adam out of dirt

He made Eve out of His rib

then the devil deceived her through a fib

In the cool of the day the Lord came

but they hid because they were filled with shame

They were clothe with animal skin

the Lord covered their sin

and that was the beginning of the curse

today things have gotten a lot worse

That's why the Lamb had to be slain

so the accuser of the brethren couldn't blame

Adam and Eve had a spiritual death

the sacrifice was met

Jesus Christ is the lamb that reign

Salvation is found in no other name

You need to make a decision

and get in with God's provision

In front of a cloud of witness

the devil continues to show bitterness

Don't look for love in the wrong places

because the devil deceives through many faces

We need to realize this world doesn't care

because the devil is the prince of the air

Our soul he wants to lure

Christ blood is pure and sure

Don't let your soul be hypnotized

because it's a demon in disguise

He wants to put you in chains

and inflict your soul with hurt and pain

In power and authority the Lord reigns

able to destroy all demonic chain!

Vanity

Why are we living for humanity?

Are we pursuing a life full of vanity?

Remember this life is just a vapor

are you serving this world as a waiter

Chasing the American dream

have you forgotten you are on God's team?

Life is just a flower

withering without the Son's power

Chasing earthly treasures

fulfilling our fleshly pleasures

Not realizing our worth

consumed with the things of this earth

Humanity chasing vanity

I think that is the opposite of Christianity.

Doubt

Do you really believe?

or are you being deceived?

The voices of life

bringing doubt causing strife

I know that I am saved

Christ rose from the grave

He defeated death

and in my soul is God's breath

I will not be double minded

confused shackled or blinded

When we are consumed by our doubts

We are no longer on God's route

Difficult is the way

Sons and Daughters please do not go astray

only the Shepherd's voice will we heed

because of His implanted Seed

The incorruptible word

Everything else is absurd.

Depression

---❦---

When trouble has consumed the heart
we must not pretend and play the part
That is the path to being depressed
you make it seem that you are blessed
but inside you can't go on
everything is going wrong
Jesus wants to take your load
will you choose the narrow road?
Broad is the way to destruction
will you not heed Jesus instruction
You and I were not made to be alone
so bow to your knees and cry out to the throne
Make your petitions be known
so the glory of God will be shown
Surrender in prayer every thing
All praises to our Lord and King.

Fear

---❦---

God has not given me a spirit of fear
so what is keeping me from drawing near?
We must take an evaluation
or else end up with frustration
Wishing you would be active
instead you are making excuses and being distracted
We are our own enemy
Christ's love is the remedy
In Christ there is a sound mind
so leave the fear behind
My mind I clothe in Christ
because He paid the ultimate sacrifice
The Holy Spirit has given me power
and I will not be devoured
In Christ I can do all things
my Savior the king of kings
So tell the fear to be quiet
And start a holly riot.

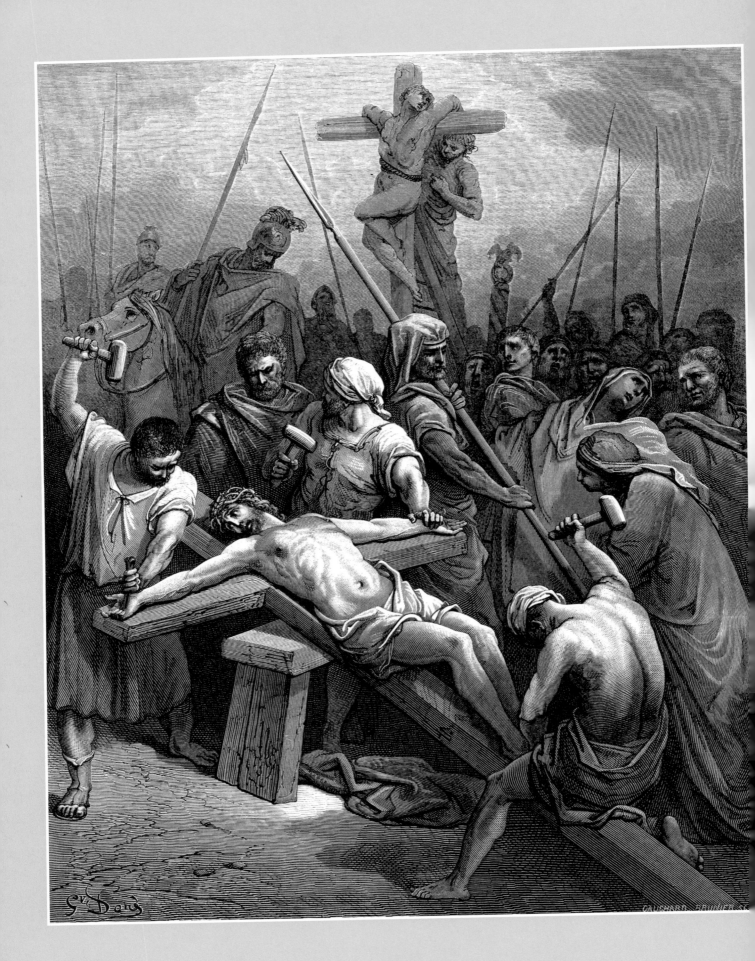

Hate

Why do we hate?
because we fall for the bait
Refusing to care for our neighbor
choosing the fruit of our own labor
Allowing the heart to be a stone
you will end up alone and disowned
God died and loved others
remember He kissed Judas my brothers
When we don't walk in love and forgiveness
we are not about the Father business
God has given us the ministry of reconciliation
that is the Gospel foundation
The opposite of hate is love
so put it aside for the sake of the one who is above
The good news is the Gospel
communicated in love not being hostile
Love covers a multitude of sins
Christ shedding His blood even His skin.
We say we love God and end up hating one another
Come on sisters and brothers
together lets unite
for the Gospel and fight.

Pride

Pride comes before a fall

it will disqualify the call

What Is the consequences of pride?

being excluded from Christ bride

We must remain humble

so our faith will not crumble

Being full of one self

will place yourself on God's shelf

Don't pat yourself on the back

according to God that is wack

Do good to others

not only your sisters and brothers

If your desire is God's grace

stay humble and seek His face

God resists the proud

so stop boasting to the crowd

Don't let wisdom puff you up

stay humble it is partaking of Christ cup.

Hope

Life is nothing but a breath

while it is day, choose life or death

Looking through the window of my eyes

I see the hurt in disguise

We hide our hurt and pain

and our souls become lame

If we allow our emotions to be suppressed

it's inevitable for our life to be oppressed

Life is nothing but a breath

while it is day choose life or death

The devil has various tools

so don't let him play us like fools

We must seek understanding and wisdom

from the one who brought us His kingdom

Don't be ignorant to the devil's ways

cause Christ promises us brighter days

The devil comes as an angel of light

but Christ gives us insight

Everyday of life we must make a choice

With our actions and our voice.

Courage

I refuse to go to hell

even though in the garden Adam fell

I understand He made me the head

and now I'm spiritually lead

The gates of hell will not prevail

I'm no longer the tail

Christ has made me a joint heir

and by His spirit I draw near

I've been risen in heavenly places

I'm no longer tormented by demons faces

Christ reigns in heaven and the earth

and we will reign with Him because of the new birth

Christ is coming as a thief in the night

soldiers lets continue to fight

Don't be caught sleeping

because the consequences will be weeping

We must abide in the vine

in order to be filled with the new wine

Don't be mislead or

you might end up spiritually dead.

Peace

In the midst of a trial
our minds run wild
Jesus left us His peace
so all worries would cease
We should seek those things that are heavenly
because they are endlessly
The bible encourages us to enter Christ rest
in spite of the tests we are blessed
On Him we cast our cares
because He has made us heirs
I am abiding in the vine
so that I may stay aligned
Not being distressed
because in the throne I have access
Christ the author and finisher of my faith
on Him I patiently wait.

Faith

---◆---

In spite of our emotions
we will stay committed to our devotions
In spite of our doubt
we will continue to shout
The race isn't given to the swift
stay focus on Christ the gift
We have to abide in the vine
and let the Holy Spirit fill us with the new wine
No need to be in a hurry just wait
knowing that God requires our faith
We must continue to press
even though all around us is a mess
We have to leave it all on this earthly field
expressing faith as our shield
Quenching all fiery darts
from corrupting good intentions of the heart
Looking unto Jesus Christ the High Priest
letting Him increase as we decrease
We will continue to make His praises known
As we continue to journey home!

Love

What is love?
Christ coming from above
In spite of our conditions
He broke all our traditions
Instead of living
He passionately expressed giving
Love never displays a parade
because love isn't a masquerade
Love never boasts
because love is just the host
Love is never jealous
because love is busy being zealous
Love is always patient
because love is ancient
Love remembers no wrongs
because it doesn't belong
Love will never cease
Just asked the prince of peace.